SCHOLASTIC

10 Vocabulary Card Games

Reproducible, Easy-to-Play Card and Board Games That Boost Kids' Vocabulary Skills — and Help Them Succeed on Tests

bright ideas™
**from
Elaine Richard**

NEW YORK • TORONTO • LONDON • AUCKLAND • SYDNEY
MEXICO CITY • NEW DELHI • HONG KONG • BUENOS AIRES

Teaching *Resources*

Dedication

These games are dedicated to:

all the children who worked with me over the
past 20 years to acquire good vocabulary skills;

my three grandchildren—Katie, Sam, and Jake—
who played these games with me just for the fun of it;

the teachers, tutors, and parents dedicated to helping
every student achieve to the highest;

Andrea and Mark for their patient and indispensable computer tutoring;

and, of course, to Jack, for his patience, advice, and encouragement.

Cover and interior design by Holly Grundon
Illustrations by Kelly Kennedy

ISBN 0-439-51378-2
Copyright © 2005 by Elaine Richard
All rights reserved.
Printed in the U.S.A.

8 9 10   40   15 14 13

Contents

Introduction

A rich vocabulary is the cornerstone of successful reading, writing, and speaking. So how can we help students develop and expand their vocabulary? One option is to offer them engaging ways to "experience" words. Enter *10 Vocabulary Card Games*! The games in this book help boost students' vocabulary—by giving them the kind of activities they'll enjoy doing over and over again. As students play these super-fun games, they gain a better understanding of synonyms, antonyms, homonyms and homophones, prefixes and root words, idioms, and more.

Setting Up the Games

M ost of the games require nothing more than the cards provided. Simply photocopy the game cards on cardstock, cut them apart, and store them in a plastic zipper bag along with a copy of the game instructions. Label the bag with the name of the game and store the bag in a filing box for easy access.

A few of the games, like "The Category Is . . . ," come with their own game boards. Some of these game boards, like the ones for Analogies Analysis and Idiomatics, may also be used with some of the other card games. Photocopy the game boards on regular copy paper then glue the pages to the inside of a manila folder, carefully aligning both sides of the game board. You could also photocopy the game board on cardstock and tape the two sides together. Consider laminating the game boards or covering them with clear plastic to keep them clean and sturdy for repeated use.

Playing the Games

The games in this book are designed for two to four players. A few can also be played at the board in a whole-class setting or in teams. You may want to establish some simple rules when you first introduce the games to avoid potential conflicts later on. For example, a quick solution to the question of who goes first is to have the youngest player always go first in a game, then play can move in a clockwise direction. A more traditional method would be to have players throw a number cube (or die) and the player with the highest number goes first. Then play continues in a clockwise direction.

Students might also play a game as "solitaire." In this case, the player writes the answers on a sheet of paper and hands it to you when he or she is finished. This could serve as an assessment tool to give you insight into the student's understanding.

Consider making the games part of the reading center or offering them as a choice during free time. You might also select a game to play with small reading groups, supervising the game to ensure appropriate answers. (Most of the games are open-ended and don't require exact answers. We provide possible answers for most games at the back of this book. You can photocopy the answer keys and give them to players to use for reference. Remind students that these are only possible answers. Accept any reasonable answers as long as players can justify them.)

Perhaps more effective than any of these options is to play the games in a one-on-one setting with an adult and a student, especially if the student needs extra help in any of the skills. A parent, teacher, or tutor can model more precise or interesting answers than peers might. Consider sending home copies of the games so students can play them with their families—another great way to strengthen the home–school connection.

However you decide to use the games in this book, they're sure to provide lots of fun and learning. Enjoy!

YR WRDS

Players list as many words as possible using two or more consonants and inserting vowels as needed.

Objective

To expand students' vocabulary, practice spelling, enhance word recognition, and develop flexibility in thinking

Players

1 or more players
(Single players can write their answers on a sheet of paper. For a whole-class game, divide the class into teams of 3 or 4 students. Write words suggested by each team on the board.)

You'll Need

- YR WRDS cards* (pages 8–11)
- Paper and pencil (for each player or team)
- Timer (optional)

* The letters Q, X, and Z were omitted because of their infrequent occurrence.

How to Play

1. Shuffle the "YR WRDS" cards and deal 3 to 5 cards to each player or team.

2. Using only the consonants they have, players list as many words as possible that can be formed by inserting vowels. (You may want to use a timer and set a time limit, like 30 seconds or 1 minute.) Players can use each consonant card only once in a word. Words with double consonants can be made only if a player gets two cards of the same consonant. For example, with the letters *R*, *D*, and *S* a player could make *ride*, *rode*, *road*, *raid*, *said*, *side*, *dries*, and so on.

3. The player or team with the most words at the end of the game wins.

10 Vocabulary Card Games   Scholastic Teaching Resources

YR WRDS

B

YR WRDS

D

YR WRDS

F

YR WRDS

B

YR WRDS

D

YR WRDS

F

YR WRDS

C

YR WRDS

D

YR WRDS

G

YR WRDS

C

YR WRDS

D

YR WRDS

G

YR WRDS	YR WRDS	YR WRDS
H	**K**	**L**
YR WRDS	YR WRDS	YR WRDS
H	**K**	**L**
YR WRDS	YR WRDS	YR WRDS
J	**L**	**M**
YR WRDS	YR WRDS	YR WRDS
J	**L**	**M**

M

N

R

N

P

R

N

P

R

N

P

R

YR WRDS

S

YR WRDS

T

YR WRDS

V

YR WRDS

S

YR WRDS

T

YR WRDS

W

YR WRDS

S

YR WRDS

T

YR WRDS

W

YR WRDS

S

YR WRDS

T

YR WRDS

Y

Match Me If You Can

> **Players match two or three word cards
> that have the same meaning.**

Objective

To help students recognize synonyms
and expand their vocabulary

Players

2 to 4 players

You'll Need

- Match Me If You Can cards
  (pages 13–16)

How to Play

1. Shuffle the "Match Me If You Can" cards. Deal the cards evenly among the players,
placing them facedown in front of each player.

2. Players turn over two cards at the same time, placing them faceup in front of them.
The first player to spot two word cards that have the same meaning can take them. If
no matches are available, players turn over another two cards and place them next to
the other cards. Words that have asterisks (∗) are part of a three-of-a-kind set. That
means that there are three cards that are synonyms. Asterisked word cards must
remain faceup until all three words are found.

3. Play continues until all cards have been matched. The player with the most cards at
the end of the game wins.

Match Me If You Can

disaster

Match Me If You Can

extra

Match Me If You Can

calamity

Match Me If You Can

additional

Match Me If You Can

float

Match Me If You Can

caution

Match Me If You Can

drift

Match Me If You Can

warning

Match Me If You Can

expand

Match Me If You Can

completely

Match Me If You Can

enlarge

Match Me If You Can

entirely

Match Me If You Can	Match Me If You Can
copy	below
Match Me If You Can	Match Me If You Can
imitate	under
Match Me If You Can	Match Me If You Can
create	boast
Match Me If You Can	Match Me If You Can
invent	brag
Match Me If You Can	Match Me If You Can
focus	explode
Match Me If You Can	Match Me If You Can
concentrate	burst

Match Me If You Can

ruin

Match Me If You Can

danger

Match Me If You Can

spoil

Match Me If You Can

peril

Match Me If You Can

sorrow

Match Me If You Can

glossy

Match Me If You Can

sadness

Match Me If You Can

shiny

Match Me If You Can

permission

Match Me If You Can

mighty

Match Me If You Can

consent

Match Me If You Can

powerful

* humorous *

* usually *

* funny *

* mostly *

* witty *

* generally *

* gigantic *

* glad *

* huge *

* happy *

* enormous *

* pleased *

Opposites Attract

In this Concentration–like game, players match two word cards that have the opposite meanings.

Objective

To help students recognize antonyms and expand their vocabulary

Players

2 to 4 players

You'll Need

- Opposites Attract cards (pages 18–21)

How to Play

1. Shuffle the "Opposites Attract" cards. Arrange the cards facedown in rows of six on a table or floor.

2. Players take turns turning over two cards at a time. If a player turns over two word cards that have opposite meanings, the player keeps the cards and gets another turn. Otherwise, the player turns the cards back facedown and the next player takes a turn.

3. Play continues until all of the cards have been matched. The player with the most cards at the end of the game wins.

Opposites Attract	Opposites Attract
fact	cheerful
Opposites Attract	Opposites Attract
fiction	gloomy
Opposites Attract	Opposites Attract
adore	costly
Opposites Attract	Opposites Attract
detest	cheap
Opposites Attract	Opposites Attract
before	danger
Opposites Attract	Opposites Attract
after	safety

Opposites Attract	Opposites Attract
doubtful	arrive
Opposites Attract	Opposites Attract
certain	depart
Opposites Attract	Opposites Attract
elderly	exit
Opposites Attract	Opposites Attract
youthful	entrance
Opposites Attract	Opposites Attract
lively	remember
Opposites Attract	Opposites Attract
dull	forget

Opposites Attract	Opposites Attract
simple	beginning
Opposites Attract	Opposites Attract
complicated	ending
Opposites Attract	Opposites Attract
victory	hazy
Opposites Attract	Opposites Attract
defeat	clear
Opposites Attract	Opposites Attract
whisper	rough
Opposites Attract	Opposites Attract
shout	smooth

Opposites Attract	Opposites Attract
calm	loosen
Opposites Attract	Opposites Attract
excited	tighten
Opposites Attract	Opposites Attract
shallow	accept
Opposites Attract	Opposites Attract
deep	reject
Opposites Attract	Opposites Attract
hastily	mighty
Opposites Attract	Opposites Attract
slowly	weak

Word Rummy

> **Players match sets of three or four synonym cards to get "Word Rummy."**

Objective

To help students recognize synonyms and enrich their vocabulary

Players

2 to 4 players

You'll Need

- Word Rummy cards (pages 23–26)

How to Play

1. Shuffle the "Word Rummy" cards and deal seven cards to each player. Stack the rest of the cards facedown and place the top card faceup next to the stack.

2. On each turn, a player may take either the faceup card or the top card from the deck, then discard a card from her hand. (Place the discarded card on top of the faceup pile.) Players must always have seven cards in their hands. The goal is to get "Word Rummy"—a set of four matching synonym cards and a second set of three matching synonym cards.

   For example, say two of a player's cards have the words *speak* and *talk*, and the faceup card has the word *utter*. The player should take the faceup card because it is a synonym of two of her cards. She then decides which of her other cards to discard. Most likely, it would be a card that doesn't match any of the others.

3. Play continues with players taking turns picking and discarding cards. The first player to get "Word Rummy" wins.

10 Vocabulary Card Games   Scholastic Teaching Resources

Word Rummy	Word Rummy
separated	**private**
Word Rummy	Word Rummy
split	**concealed**
Word Rummy	Word Rummy
divided	**assembly**
Word Rummy	Word Rummy
apart	**gathering**
Word Rummy	Word Rummy
secret	**meeting**
Word Rummy	Word Rummy
hidden	**group**

Word Rummy	Word Rummy
fearless	**repair**
Word Rummy	Word Rummy
unafraid	**patch**
Word Rummy	Word Rummy
bold	**say**
Word Rummy	Word Rummy
daring	**speak**
Word Rummy	Word Rummy
fix	**announce**
Word Rummy	Word Rummy
mend	**tell**

Word Rummy

connect

Word Rummy

price

Word Rummy

unite

Word Rummy

amount

Word Rummy

combine

Word Rummy

sleep

Word Rummy

meld

Word Rummy

doze

Word Rummy

charges

Word Rummy

nap

Word Rummy

cost

Word Rummy

slumber

Word Rummy	Word Rummy
only	instruct
Word Rummy	**Word Rummy**
sole	educate
Word Rummy	**Word Rummy**
unique	entire
Word Rummy	**Word Rummy**
singular	all
Word Rummy	**Word Rummy**
teach	total
Word Rummy	**Word Rummy**
inform	whole

Many Meanings

> ## Players use a word in two or more sentences to demonstrate its different meanings.

Objective

To enhance precise use of vocabulary by giving students experience in using *homonyms* (words that are spelled and pronounced the same but have different meanings) in different sentences

Players

2 to 4 players

You'll Need

- Many Meanings cards (pages 28–31)

Optional Materials

- Game board (choose one from pages 54–55 or 66–67)
- Game markers (buttons or coins work well)

How to Play

1. Shuffle the "Many Meanings" cards and stack them facedown between the players.

2. Players take turns picking a card from the pile. On each turn, a player reads aloud the word on the card and uses the word in at least two sentences to show its different meanings. For example, the word *light* can be used in the following sentences: *I turned on the* light. *She's wearing a* light *shade of blue. The suitcase was* light, *not heavy.*

3. Score one point for two meanings, and two points for each additional meaning. (In the example above, the score would be 4.)

4. Continue taking turns until no cards are left. The player with the most points at the end of the game wins.

Playing with a Game Board

Each player places a marker on START. Play the game as described above. A player can move forward one space for giving two meanings, and two extra spaces for each additional meaning. The first person to reach FINISH wins.

10 Vocabulary Card Games   Scholastic Teaching Resources

1	Many Meanings	7	Many Meanings
	back		can

2	Many Meanings	8	Many Meanings
	ball		cast

3	Many Meanings	9	Many Meanings
	bat		cold

4	Many Meanings	10	Many Meanings
	blue		fair

5	Many Meanings	11	Many Meanings
	break		file

6	Many Meanings	12	Many Meanings
	bug		fine

13 Many Meanings

fly

14 Many Meanings

hand

15 Many Meanings

hard

16 Many Meanings

head

17 Many Meanings

hide

18 Many Meanings

left

19 Many Meanings

light

20 Many Meanings

log

21 Many Meanings

may

22 Many Meanings

mean

23 Many Meanings

might

24 Many Meanings

nail

25 Many Meanings order	**31** Many Meanings safe
26 Many Meanings past	**32** Many Meanings scale
27 Many Meanings pen	**33** Many Meanings seal
28 Many Meanings present	**34** Many Meanings season
29 Many Meanings punch	**35** Many Meanings set
30 Many Meanings ring	**36** Many Meanings sign

37 Many Meanings	43 Many Meanings
sink	tail
38 Many Meanings	44 Many Meanings
space	tape
39 Many Meanings	45 Many Meanings
spot	tie
40 Many Meanings	46 Many Meanings
stick	top
41 Many Meanings	47 Many Meanings
strike	type
42 Many Meanings	48 Many Meanings
swing	watch

Hippy Homophones

After a sentence is read aloud to a player, the player must spell or define the homophone correctly.

Objective

To help students understand the correct use of homophones in reading and writing

Players

2 to 4 players

You'll Need

- Hippy Homophones cards (pages 33–36)

How to Play

1. Shuffle the "Hippy Homophones" cards and stack them facedown between players.

2. On each player's turn, the person to the right of the player picks a card and reads aloud the word at the top of the card and the sentence below it. The player then has to spell or define the word that was used in the sentence. For example, say the word at the top of the card is *eight* and the sentence reads: ***Laura found eight coins in the playground.*** The player has to spell the word *eight* or define it *(the number)*.

3. If the player answers correctly, he keeps the card. If not, the player to his left can try to spell or define the word. If that player answers correctly, she keeps the card and takes another turn.

4. Play continues until no cards are left. The person with the most cards at the end of the game wins.

10 Vocabulary Card Games   Scholastic Teaching Resources

Hippy Homophones

Ad
Did you see the new <u>ad</u>
for that cool car?

Hippy Homophones

Dew
The <u>dew</u> on that rose petal looks
almost like a diamond.

Hippy Homophones

Add
If you <u>add</u> these two numbers correctly,
you'll get the answer you need.

Hippy Homophones

Due
Your library book is <u>due</u>
next Thursday.

Hippy Homophones

Aisle
The bride looked so lovely as
she walked down the <u>aisle</u>.

Hippy Homophones

Break
I could use a <u>break</u> from
all this work.

Hippy Homophones

I'll
<u>I'll</u> see you next week
when I return.

Hippy Homophones

Brake
Jaime tested the <u>brake</u> on his bike
to make sure it was working.

Hippy Homophones

Isle
I wonder what it would be like
to live on a deserted <u>isle</u>.

Hippy Homophones

Ceiling
Mom put some glow-in-the-dark
stars on our bedroom <u>ceiling</u>.

Hippy Homophones

Do
Kia and Alex <u>do</u> all the work here.

Hippy Homophones

Sealing
Charles is <u>sealing</u> the envelope.

Hippy Homophones

Cheap

Even on sale, that sweater is not <u>cheap</u>.

Hippy Homophones

Mail

Could you please pick up the <u>mail</u> from the post office?

Hippy Homophones

Cheep

I can hear the little chicks <u>cheep</u> in the barn.

Hippy Homophones

Male

The vet said that the stray cat is a <u>male</u>.

Hippy Homophones

Desert

Are you going to <u>desert</u> your friends, too?

Hippy Homophones

Meat

Sarah is trying to eat less <u>meat</u> and more fruits and vegetables.

Hippy Homophones

Dessert

Lana ate all the <u>dessert</u> left in the refrigerator.

Hippy Homophones

Meet

Let's <u>meet</u> at the mall tomorrow afternoon.

Hippy Homophones

Groan

When Jeremy heard there was going to be a test, he just had to <u>groan</u>.

Hippy Homophones

Pail

The twins always bring their shovel and <u>pail</u> to the beach.

Hippy Homophones

Grown

You have <u>grown</u> so much since I last saw you.

Hippy Homophones

Pale

Kevin looked so <u>pale</u>, you'd think he had seen a ghost.

Hippy Homophones

Pause

When you read the poem,
<u>pause</u> after each line.

Hippy Homophones

Rose

Stella gave her mother a single
<u>rose</u> for her birthday.

Hippy Homophones

Paws

The dog's <u>paws</u> are so muddy!

Hippy Homophones

Rows

All the <u>rows</u> in the
stadium are filled up.

Hippy Homophones

Peace

Now that those kids are gone, we
can have some <u>peace</u> and quiet.

Hippy Homophones

Stair

We'll climb all the way to the top,
one <u>stair</u> at a time.

Hippy Homophones

Piece

Would you like a <u>piece</u> of cake?

Hippy Homophones

Stare

Jack couldn't help but
<u>stare</u> at her hair.

Hippy Homophones

Roll

In shock, Dad watched the car
<u>roll</u> down the hill.

Hippy Homophones

Tail

Watch out for the cat's <u>tail</u>!

Hippy Homophones

Role

What <u>role</u> would you like to
play in this year's production?

Hippy Homophones

Tale

Have you heard the <u>tale</u> about
the giant lumberjack?

Hippy Homophones

Tied
Juan <u>tied</u> his boat to the dock.

Hippy Homophones

Weak
Kendra felt <u>weak</u> from the flu.

Hippy Homophones

Tide
Sometimes you can walk far out into the ocean when the <u>tide</u> is low.

Hippy Homophones

Week
We're going on vacation next <u>week</u>.

Hippy Homophones

Throne
Prince Charles is next in line to the <u>throne</u> of England.

Hippy Homophones

Weather
Have you checked tomorrow's <u>weather</u>?

Hippy Homophones

Thrown
If you hadn't <u>thrown</u> away the map, we'd know where to go.

Hippy Homophones

Whether
I don't know <u>whether</u> or not to join the team.

Hippy Homophones

Wait
I'll <u>wait</u> for you at the bus stop.

Hippy Homophones

Which
<u>Which</u> do you prefer—pizza or hot dog?

Hippy Homophones

Weight
Tomas lost all the <u>weight</u> he gained during Thanksgiving.

Hippy Homophones

Witch
Glinda is the good <u>witch</u> in *The Wizard of Oz*.

The Category Is ...

> **Players write a number of words that belong in a specific category.**

Objective

To help enhance students' word retrieval and expand their vocabulary

Players

2 players, or 2 teams with 2 players each

You'll Need

- Set of The Category Is . . . cards* (choose one set from pages 38–41)
- Game board (pages 42–43)
- Paper clip and pencil (for the spinner)
- Categories answer sheet (page 44)
- Pencils
- Timer (optional)

* You may want to copy the Categories cards onto self-adhesive notes so that they stay in place on the game board.

How to Play

1. Choose one set of cards and place a card on each "station" on the game board. Distribute the answer sheet and a pencil to each player.

2. Starting at the first station, a player spins the spinner to determine how many words to write that belong to a category. For example, say a player spins 5 and the category is *Pets*. Each player must list five words that belong to that category. (You may want to use a timer and set a time limit, like 30 seconds or 1 minute.)

3. Play continues as players move to the next station and take turns spinning the spinner.

4. After everyone has completed all the stations, players compare answers for each category. Cross out any answers that are the same as other players'. Count the remaining words. The player with the most words wins.

Set 1	Set 2
The Category Is ...	**The Category Is ...**
transportation	musical instruments
Set 1	Set 2
The Category Is ...	**The Category Is ...**
summer words	shapes
Set 1	Set 2
The Category Is ...	**The Category Is ...**
vegetables	tools
Set 1	Set 2
The Category Is ...	**The Category Is ...**
computer words	school
Set 1	Set 2
The Category Is ...	**The Category Is ...**
sports	artists
Set 1	Set 2
The Category Is ...	**The Category Is ...**
baby animals	flowers

Set 3
The Category Is ...

winter words

Set 4
The Category Is ...

bodies of water

Set 3
The Category Is ...

feelings

Set 4
The Category Is ...

round things

Set 3
The Category Is ...

toys

Set 4
The Category Is ...

weather

Set 3
The Category Is ...

wild animals

Set 4
The Category Is ...

foreign languages

Set 3
The Category Is ...

medical terms

Set 4
The Category Is ...

flavors

Set 3
The Category Is ...

fruits

Set 4
The Category Is ...

clothing

Set 5 The Category Is ...	Set 6 The Category Is ...
kitchen	**measurement**
Set 5 The Category Is ...	Set 6 The Category Is ...
farm	**camera words**
Set 5 The Category Is ...	Set 6 The Category Is ...
furniture	**sharp things**
Set 5 The Category Is ...	Set 6 The Category Is ...
green things	**soft things**
Set 5 The Category Is ...	Set 6 The Category Is ...
playground	**insects**
Set 5 The Category Is ...	Set 6 The Category Is ...
colors	**things made of glass**

Set 7 The Category Is ... (**things that fly**)	**Set 8** The Category Is ... (**things you read**)
Set 7 The Category Is ... (**things in a supermarket**)	**Set 8** The Category Is ... (**sounds**)
Set 7 The Category Is ... (**desserts**)	**Set 8** The Category Is ... (**planets**)
Set 7 The Category Is ... (**small things**)	**Set 8** The Category Is ... (**movement words**)
Set 7 The Category Is ... (**vacation destinations**)	**Set 8** The Category Is ... (**things made of paper**)
Set 7 The Category Is ... (**landforms**)	**Set 8** The Category Is ... (**body parts**)

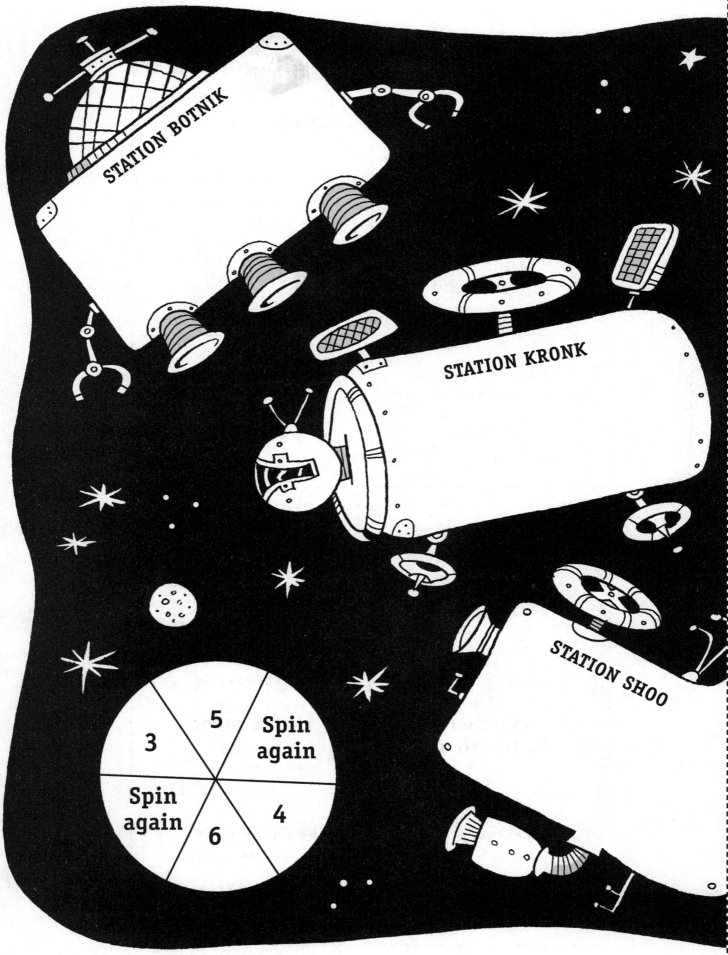

Categories Answer Sheet

Category:_____

1. _____
2. _____
3. _____
4. _____
5. _____
6. _____

Categories Answer Sheet

Category:_____

1. _____
2. _____
3. _____
4. _____
5. _____
6. _____

Categories Answer Sheet

Category:_____

1. _____
2. _____
3. _____
4. _____
5. _____
6. _____

Categories Answer Sheet

Category:_____

1. _____
2. _____
3. _____
4. _____
5. _____
6. _____

Categories Answer Sheet

Category:_____

1. _____
2. _____
3. _____
4. _____
5. _____
6. _____

Categories Answer Sheet

Category:_____

1. _____
2. _____
3. _____
4. _____
5. _____
6. _____

Roots and Prefixes Bingo

> **In this bingo-style game, a caller calls out prefixes for players to match with the root words on their cards.**

Objective

To reinforce understanding of root words and prefixes

Players

2 to 4 players, plus a caller

You'll Need

- Root Words Bingo cards (pages 46–47)
- Prefix cards (page 48)
- Envelope or small paper bag (for the Prefix cards)
- Bingo markers (coins or buttons work well)

How to Play

1. Distribute a "Root Words Bingo" card and bingo markers to each player. Cut apart the "Prefix" cards and put them in the envelope.

2. The caller picks a card from the envelope and reads the prefix aloud. Each player looks at his or her own bingo card and decides which root word goes with the prefix. For example, say the caller reads the prefix *in-* and a player has the root word ***tend*** on his card. Combined, the prefix and root word make the word ***intend***. The player should say the complete word aloud then put a marker on the word ***tend*** on his card.

3. The object of the game is to cover a complete row of four root words, vertically, horizontally, or diagonally. NOTE: There may be more than one root word for each prefix. Players should decide which root word to cover in order to get bingo.

4. The first player to get bingo wins.

10 Vocabulary Card Games   Scholastic Teaching Resources

Root Words Bingo Card

change	plain	fill	pack
build	tract	tell	pect
safe	pose	able	ject
charge	serve	please	base

Root Words Bingo Card

play	pand	cess	bate
vent	verse	form	tail
act	fair	view	cent
dict	cover	cite	test

Root Words Bingo Card

able	change	base	cite
test	charge	verse	fair
pack	play	build	form
vent	pose	serve	cent

Root Words Bingo Card

safe	act	plain	dict
fill	ject	pand	cover
tract	cess	view	tell
please	pect	bate	tail

Prefix Cards

com-	con-	con-	de-	de-
de-	di-	dis-	dis-	dis-
en-	ex-	ex-	ex-	in-
in-	per-	pre-	pro-	re-
re-	re-	re-	un-	un-

Analogies Analysis

Players fill in the blanks with appropriate analogies.

Objective

To help students explore word relationships and comparisons frequently found in literature and on standardized tests; to help them better understand metaphors in poetry and to enrich language usage in writing

Players

2 to 4 players

You'll Need

- Analogies Analysis cards (pages 50–53)
- Analogies game board (pages 54–55)
- Game markers (buttons or coins work well)
- Number cube (die)

How to Play

1. Shuffle the "Analogies Analysis" cards and stack them facedown next to the game board. Players place their markers on START.

2. On each turn, a player picks a card and reads the statement aloud. The player fills in the blank by giving an appropriate analogy. For example, say the card reads: *Horn is to beep as phone is to _____.* An appropriate analogy might be *ring*.

3. If the player answers correctly, she rolls the number cube to see how many spaces to move on the board. If the player doesn't answer correctly, the next player can try to guess the answer. If he answers correctly, he can roll the cube to move forward on the board, then take another turn.

4. Continue taking turns until one player reaches FINISH. The first person to reach FINISH wins.

10 Vocabulary Card Games   Scholastic Teaching Resources

1 Analogies Analysis

Head is to foot
as top is to _____

2 Analogies Analysis

Whisper is to shout
as quiet is to _____

3 Analogies Analysis

Money is to bank
as food is to _____

4 Analogies Analysis

Foot is to shoe
as hand is to _____

5 Analogies Analysis

Car is to drive
as pencil is to _____

6 Analogies Analysis

Computer is to process
as brain is to _____

7 Analogies Analysis

Ice is to solid
as water is to _____

8 Analogies Analysis

Red flag is to danger
as white flag is to _____

9 Analogies Analysis

Blue is to color
as carrot is to _____

10 Analogies Analysis

Win is to lose
as stop is to _____

11 Analogies Analysis

Whistle is to referee
as hammer is to _____

12 Analogies Analysis

She is to her
as he is to _____

13	Analogies Analysis
	Glass is to shatter as paper is to _____

19	Analogies Analysis
	Frog is to pond as bee is to _____

14	Analogies Analysis
	Story is to read as song is to _____

20	Analogies Analysis
	Villain is to hero as wealth is to _____

15	Analogies Analysis
	Character is to book as ingredient is to _____

21	Analogies Analysis
	Star is to galaxy as planet is to _____

16	Analogies Analysis
	Date is to calendar as time is to _____

22	Analogies Analysis
	Attract is to repel as healthy is to _____

17	Analogies Analysis
	Left is to right as front is to _____

23	Analogies Analysis
	Difficult is to hard as fragile is to _____

18	Analogies Analysis
	Tree is to lumber as wheat is to _____

24	Analogies Analysis
	Study is to learn as search is to _____

25 Analogies Analysis

Anger is to fury
as joy is to _____

31 Analogies Analysis

Fish is to swim
as bird is to _____

26 Analogies Analysis

Dog is to puppy
as cow is to _____

32 Analogies Analysis

Shelf is to books
as garage is to _____

27 Analogies Analysis

Sunshine is to rain
as happy is to _____

33 Analogies Analysis

Page is to book
as branch is to _____

28 Analogies Analysis

Bracelet is to wrist
as ring is to _____

34 Analogies Analysis

Finger is to hand
as toe is to _____

29 Analogies Analysis

Football is to touchdown
as soccer is to _____

35 Analogies Analysis

Chair is to sit
as stove is to _____

30 Analogies Analysis

Screen is to movie
as stage is to _____

36 Analogies Analysis

Ear is to listen
as tongue is to _____

37 Analogies Analysis

Engine is to go
as brake is to _____

38 Analogies Analysis

Length is to inches
as weight is to _____

39 Analogies Analysis

One is to three
as single is to _____

40 Analogies Analysis

Moon is to earth
as earth is to _____

41 Analogies Analysis

Swim is to pool
as jog is to _____

42 Analogies Analysis

Paw is to dog
as fin is to _____

43 Analogies Analysis

Silk is to smooth
as sandpaper is to _____

44 Analogies Analysis

Tame is to wild
as pretty is to _____

45 Analogies Analysis

Geometry is to math
as biology is to _____

46 Analogies Analysis

Advance is to retreat
as panic is to _____

47 Analogies Analysis

Sum is to addition
as product is to _____

48 Analogies Analysis

Tired is to sleep
as hungry is to _____

Analogies

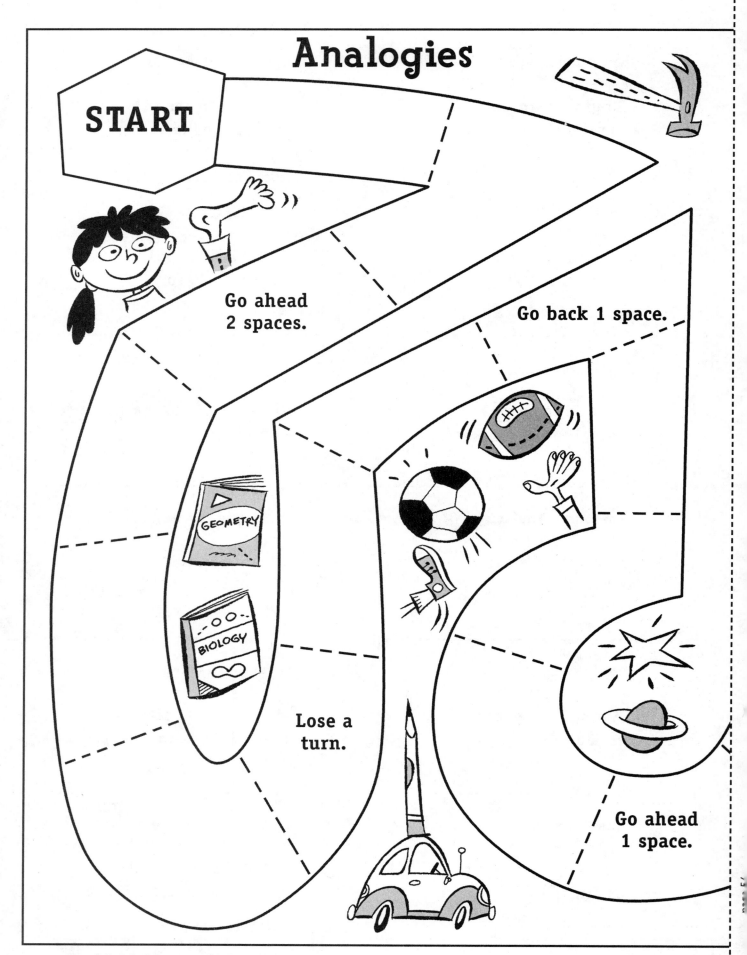

START

Go ahead 2 spaces.

Go back 1 space.

GEOMETRY

BIOLOGY

Lose a turn.

Go ahead 1 space.

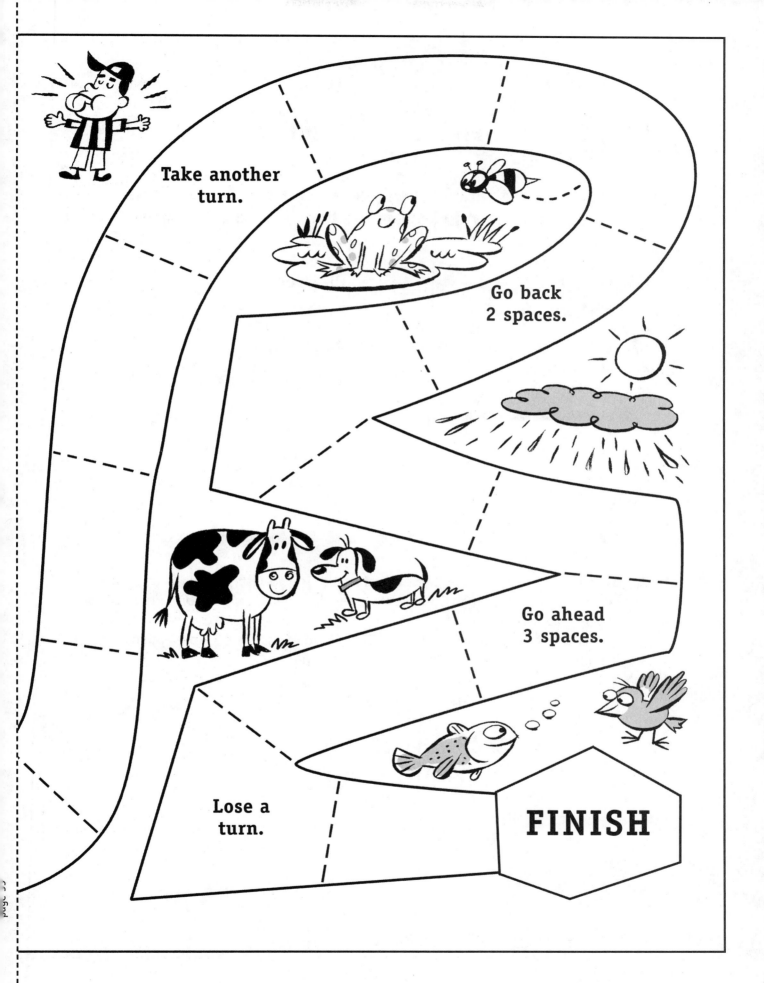

Smilin' Similes

In this Concentration-type game, players match two phrase cards to make a simile then use the simile in a sentence.

Objective

To help students recognize familiar similes (figures of speech that compare two unlike things by using the word **as** or **like**) and enrich their understanding of them

Players

2 to 4 players

You'll Need

- Smilin' Similes cards (pages 57–60)

How to Play

1. Shuffle the "Smilin' Similes" cards. Arrange the cards facedown in rows of six on a table or floor.

2. Players take turns flipping over two cards at a time. The goal is to turn over two phrase cards that, put together, make a simile (for example, the phrases **as sharp** and **as a tack**). If a player turns over two cards that make a simile, he has to use the simile in a sentence that makes sense in order to keep the cards. Otherwise, the player turns the cards back facedown and the next player takes a turn.

3. Play continues until all of the cards have been matched. The player with the most cards at the end of the game wins.

10 Vocabulary Card Games   Scholastic Teaching Resources

Smilin' Similes	Smilin' Similes
As pretty ...	As busy ...
Smilin' Similes	Smilin' Similes
As fluffy ...	Sings ...
Smilin' Similes	Smilin' Similes
Swims ...	Sleeps ...
Smilin' Similes	Smilin' Similes
As peaceful ...	Fight ...
Smilin' Similes	Smilin' Similes
As gentle ...	As flat ...
Smilin' Similes	Smilin' Similes
As slippery ...	As deep ...

Smilin' Similes

... as a picture

Smilin' Similes

... as a bee

Smilin' Similes

... as a cloud

Smilin' Similes

... like a bird

Smilin' Similes

... like a fish

Smilin' Similes

... like a baby

Smilin' Similes

... as a dove

Smilin' Similes

... like cats and dogs

Smilin' Similes

... as a lamb

Smilin' Similes

... as a pancake

Smilin' Similes

... as an eel

Smilin' Similes

... as the ocean

Smilin' Similes

As white ...

Smilin' Similes

As black ...

Smilin' Similes

As light ...

Smilin' Similes

Moves ...

Smilin' Similes

As cold ...

Smilin' Similes

As smooth ...

Smilin' Similes

Sinks ...

Smilin' Similes

As soft ...

Smilin' Similes

As strong ...

Smilin' Similes

As tall ...

Smilin' Similes

As rough ...

Smilin' Similes

As sly ...

Smilin' Similes	Smilin' Similes
... as snow	... as night
Smilin' Similes	Smilin' Similes
... as a feather	... like a snail
Smilin' Similes	Smilin' Similes
... as ice	... as glass
Smilin' Similes	Smilin' Similes
... like a stone	... as silk
Smilin' Similes	Smilin' Similes
... as a horse	... as a flagpole
Smilin' Similes	Smilin' Similes
... as sandpaper	... as a fox

Idiomatics

> **Players read a statement containing an idiom and explain what the idiom means.**

Objective

To help students understand idioms so they do not take them literally

Players

2 to 4 players

You'll Need

- Idiomatics cards (pages 62–65)

- Idioms game board (pages 66–67)

- Game markers (buttons or coins work well)

How to Play

1. Shuffle the "Idiomatics" cards and stack them facedown next to the game board. Players place their markers on START.

2. On each turn, a player picks a card and reads the statement aloud. The player then explains what the underlined idiom means.

3. If the player answers correctly, he moves the number of spaces written on the card. If the player doesn't answer correctly, he does not move. Place the card in a discard pile. The next player takes a turn.

4. The first player to reach FINISH wins.

10 Vocabulary Card Games   Scholastic Teaching Resources

1 Idiomatics

I knew she wasn't listening because her <u>head was in the clouds</u>.

(2)

2 Idiomatics

If you tell me what you need, I can get working on it <u>right off the bat</u>.

(2)

3 Idiomatics

Keenan got <u>cold feet</u> when he looked down the ski slope.

(2)

4 Idiomatics

After Sarah's team lost, she felt <u>down in the dumps</u>.

(2)

5 Idiomatics

Ann was <u>tickled pink</u> when the principal praised her project.

(3)

6 Idiomatics

Tom <u>hit the roof</u> when he found out his friend had lied to him.

(3)

7 Idiomatics

They <u>pulled strings</u> to get tickets to the sold-out Yankees game.

(3)

8 Idiomatics

As Zach told his outrageous story, Ria couldn't <u>keep a straight face</u>.

(2)

9 Idiomatics

Joe decided to go <u>out on a limb</u> and tell his parents about his report card.

(3)

10 Idiomatics

When the mayor visited our school, he got the <u>red-carpet treatment</u>.

(2)

11 Idiomatics

Everyone was feeling shy, but the party game <u>broke the ice</u>.

(3)

12 Idiomatics

Lara said she'll set up the party <u>from soup to nuts</u>.

(2)

13	Idiomatics

Be careful what you say so you won't have to <u>eat your words</u> later.

(3)

19	Idiomatics

The beach was fun, but my little brother was such a <u>wet blanket</u>.

(2)

14	Idiomatics

Mom <u>calls the shots</u> at home.

(2)

20	Idiomatics

Stop <u>making waves</u> and just go along with our original plans.

(2)

15	Idiomatics

Andrew was so embarrassed, he just <u>clammed up</u>.

(2)

21	Idiomatics

The <u>dark-horse candidate</u> was elected class president.

(3)

16	Idiomatics

Sally's baby brother is the <u>spitting image</u> of her.

(2)

22	Idiomatics

I've always put up with his jokes, but this is <u>the last straw</u>!

(3)

17	Idiomatics

Our go-cart fell apart at the trials, so now we're <u>back to square one</u>.

(3)

23	Idiomatics

Lisa didn't want her brother to get in trouble, so she <u>took the rap</u> for him.

(3)

18	Idiomatics

Don't worry about Mr. Howard— <u>his bark is worse than his bite</u>.

(3)

24	Idiomatics

Sam has been <u>on cloud nine</u> since he won first prize.

(2)

25	Idiomatics
	Krista's hope for a swimming party went <u>down the drain</u>. (2)

31	Idiomatics
	When Jim saw Jill come around the corner, he <u>took a powder</u>. (2)

26	Idiomatics
	Please <u>keep this information under your hat</u>. (2)

32	Idiomatics
	Why are you giving your best friend the <u>cold shoulder</u>? (2)

27	Idiomatics
	Just <u>hang in there</u> and you'll eventually get what you want. (3)

33	Idiomatics
	What Kim found out is just the <u>tip of the iceberg</u>. (2)

28	Idiomatics
	My grandmother's garden is proof that she has a <u>green thumb</u>. (2)

34	Idiomatics
	Carlos did not <u>hit the books</u> until the night before the test. (2)

29	Idiomatics
	Gina's teachers love her because she's <u>quick on the draw</u>. (3)

35	Idiomatics
	Since she heard the great news, Sandra has been <u>walking on air</u>. (2)

30	Idiomatics
	Let's stop this <u>monkey business</u> and get working on the project. (2)

36	Idiomatics
	If you continue to <u>burn the candle at both ends</u>, you'll make yourself sick. (3)

37 Idiomatics	**43** Idiomatics
That surprise math quiz was a <u>piece of cake</u>. (3)	Kira is tired of <u>playing second fiddle</u> to her older sister. (3)
38 Idiomatics	**44** Idiomatics
Katie passed the test <u>with flying colors</u>. (2)	Even after José lost, he really <u>kept his chin up</u>. (2)
39 Idiomatics	**45** Idiomatics
Looks like the TV is <u>on the fritz</u> again. (2)	When you said Bob has no imagination, you <u>hit the nail right on the head</u>. (3)
40 Idiomatics	**46** Idiomatics
Maya was <u>green with envy</u> when Taiyo won the spelling bee. (2)	No matter how hard he tries, Jack just <u>can't hold a candle</u> to Jake. (3)
41 Idiomatics	**47** Idiomatics
Don't bother to see that movie—it's <u>for the birds</u>. (2)	If Mom sees this mess, she'll <u>jump down your throat</u>. (3)
42 Idiomatics	**48** Idiomatics
Ian lost his job at the restaurant because he couldn't <u>cut the mustard</u>. (3)	Tam <u>spilled the beans</u> about the surprise party. (3)

START

Go ahead
2 spaces.

Go back
3 spaces.

Go ahead
2 spaces.

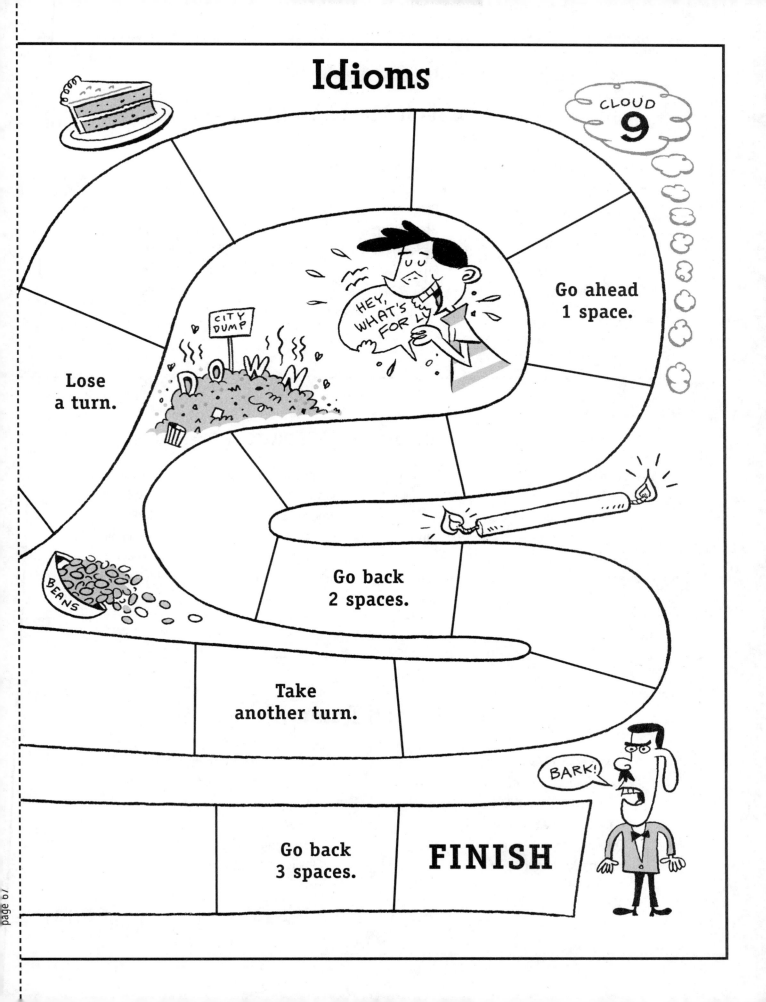

Match Me If You Can (page 12)

Possible Answers

Disaster/Calamity
Float/Drift
Expand/Enlarge
Extra/Additional
Caution/Warning
Completely/Entirely
Copy/Imitate

Create/Invent
Focus/Concentrate
Below/Under
Boast/Brag
Explode/Burst
Ruin/Spoil
Sorrow/Sadness
Permission/Consent

Danger/Peril
Glossy/Shiny
Mighty/Powerful
Humorous/Funny/Witty
Gigantic/Huge/Enormous
Usually/Mostly/Generally
Glad/Happy/Pleased

Opposites Attract (page 17)

Possible Answers

Fact/Fiction
Adore/Detest
Before/After
Cheerful/Gloomy
Costly/Cheap
Danger/Safety

Doubtful/Certain
Elderly/Youthful
Lively/Dull
Arrive/Depart
Exit/Entrance
Remember/Forget

Simple/Complicated
Victory/Defeat
Whisper/Shout
Beginning/Ending
Hazy/Clear
Rough/Smooth

Calm/Excited
Shallow/Deep
Hastily/Slowly
Loosen/Tighten
Accept/Reject
Mighty/Weak

Word Rummy (page 22)

Possible Answers

Separated/Split/Divided/Apart
Secret/Hidden/Private/Concealed
Assembly/Gathering/Meeting/Group
Fearless/Unafraid/Bold/Daring
Fix/Mend/Repair/Patch
Say/Speak/Announce/Tell

Connect/Unite/Combine/Meld
Charges/Cost/Price/Amount
Sleep/Doze/Nap/Slumber
Only/Sole/Unique/Singular
Teach/Inform/Instruct/Educate
Entire/All/Total/Whole

1. Back – rear part of the body; opposite of *front*; position in some ball games, like football or soccer; toward the rear; in the past; having returned from somewhere; to support, as in *back up someone*; to move backward

2. Ball – a round plaything; a large formal party; a good time, as in *having a ball*

3. Bat – a flying mammal; a stick used in baseball; to hit a ball with a bat; flutter, as in *bat eyelashes*

4. Blue – a color; feeling sad

5. Break – to destroy something; to split something into smaller parts; a rest from school or work, like a vacation

6. Bug – an insect or other creepy crawly; to annoy someone; to plant a hidden microphone, as in *bug a house*

7. Can – to be able to do; a metallic cylinder for holding food; to put in a can

8. Cast – players in a show; bandages with plaster used for broken arms or legs; to throw something, as in *cast a stone*; to give shape to something, like pottery

9. Cold – low temperature; opposite of *warm*; illness caused by viruses; not friendly

10. Fair – light coloring; not dark; just or reasonable, as in *a fair trial*; average; beauty; an exhibition of products or trade show

11. File – a tool used to smooth surfaces; to arrange papers in order; collection of data in a computer

12. Fine – feel well; penalty paid as punishment; very thin or delicate, such as *fine thread*

13. Fly – a winged insect; the act of flying, like a bird; a baseball hit high in the air

14. Hand – part of the arm; help or assistance, as in *give a hand*; applause; a worker on a ship, as in *all hands on deck*; near, as in *at hand*

15. Hard – difficult; opposite of *soft*; harsh, as in *a hard person*

16. Head – topmost part of the body; leader or person in charge, as in *head of the class*; to move toward a certain direction, as in *head for home*

17. Hide – to put something out of sight; to keep something secret; the skin of an animal

18. Left – opposite of *right*; past tense of *leave*

19. Light – electromagnetic radiation that's visible to the eye, as in daylight or from a lightbulb; bright; opposite of *dark*; opposite of *heavy*; to illuminate; food with less calories, as in *light salad dressing*

20. Log – a large piece of wood, specifically a cut section of a tree trunk; a record of a ship or plane's voyage; a daily record of events

21. May – the fifth month in a year; be able to do something

22. Mean – to have a purpose, as in *she means to get rich*; to denote something, as in *hungry means needing to eat something*; nasty, as in *he was mean to her*; average, as in math; poor

23. Might – another word for *may*; power or strength

24. Nail – hard covering at the end of fingers and toes; a pointed metal fastener, used with a hammer

25. Order – arrangement or sequence, as in *put something in order*; to command, as in *order the troops*; rank or level

26. Past – time gone by; opposite of *present*; go by and beyond a place, as in *drive past the school*

27. Pen – a writing utensil; an enclosure to hold in animals, as in a *pig pen*; a female swan

28. Present – now; opposite of *past*; a gift; here, as in *present in school*

29. Punch – a drink that is a mixture of different juices or liquids; to push down, as in *punch keys on the computer*; to hit someone with a fist

30. Ring – a circular piece of jewelry, usually worn on a finger; sound usually made by a bell; to surround in a circle, as in *ring around the rosy*

31. Safe – free from harm; a case for putting valuables, like jewelry

32. Scale – a device for weighing; to climb, as in *scale a wall*; the outer covering of fish; a series of consecutive musical notes

33. Seal – a sea mammal; to close, as in *seal an envelope*

34. Season – a period of time during the year, as in *spring season*; to add seasoning, like salt, to food

35. Set – a collection of things that belong together, as in *a train set*; to place somewhere, as in *set the bowl on the table*; to harden something, as in *let the gelatin set*

36. Sign – a symbol or omen; to write a signature, as in *sign your name*; a type of display, usually to advertise something; to signal someone

37. Sink – to go under the surface, as in *sink to the bottom*; a basin, as in a kitchen or bathroom sink

38. Space – the universe, as in *outer space*; room, as in *space to spread out*; leave a gap in between, as in *space out your letters*

39. Spot – a stain; a small area that's a different color from its surroundings, such as spots on a Dalmatian; a small space; a brief commercial; to see or notice something, as in *spot a mistake*

40. Stick – a long piece of wood or a broken branch; to fasten something as with paste or glue; to place something somewhere, as in *stick it in the drawer*

41. Strike – to hit or attack; to delete or cancel, as in *strike that last word*; a work stoppage by employees, as in *go on strike*

42. Swing – a playground equipment; to sway back and forth; a type of jazz music

43. Tail – an appendage at an animal's rear end; to follow secretly, as in *tail a suspect*; a comet's bright, trailing end

44. Tape – an adhesive strip, as in *Scotch tape*; an audiotape; to record something on tape

45. Tie – a necktie; to fasten using ribbon or string; an equal score in a game

46. Top – the highest or uppermost part of something; a spinning toy; the best; to exceed something; to cover, as in *top a sundae with cherry*

47. Type – kind or sort, as in *a type of animal*; printed letters, as in a *typeface*; to write something using a keyboard

48. Watch – to keep an eye on or to observe; a device that tells time, like a clock; to be careful about something, as in *watch out for danger*

Hippy Homophones (page 32)

Ad – advertisement

Add – to calculate the sum

Aisle – a passage separating sections of seats

I'll – I will

Isle – island

Do – to carry out

Dew – moisture that appears as small droplets

Due – date at which something is required

Break – period of rest

Brake – a device for stopping motion

Ceiling – overhead part of a room

Sealing – closing

Cheap – inexpensive

Cheep – sound made by little chicks

Desert – leave behind (Note that the accent is on the second syllable, as opposed to *desert* that means "dry land.")

Dessert – sweet treat after a meal

Groan – to make a deep moaning sound

Grown – having matured or gotten taller

Mail – letters

Male – boy or man; masculine

Meat – animal flesh, like beef, pork, or chicken

Meet – to come together

Pail – a container, like a bucket

Pale – lacking in color

Pause – stop briefly

Paws – an animal's feet

Peace – calm or quiet

Piece – part of a whole

Roll – to move, as on wheels

Role – an acting part in a play

Rose – a flower

Rows – arranged in straight lines

Stair – step

Stare – to look hard

Tail – an appendage at the back of many animals

Tale – story

Tied – to fasten with a rope

Tide – the rising and falling of the ocean

Throne – chair of state of a sovereign, like a king or queen

Thrown – past tense of *throw*

Wait – to stay in place, expecting something to come

Weight – how much a person weighs

Weak – not strong

Week – seven-day cycle from Sunday to Saturday

Weather – state of the atmosphere, like rainy or sunny

Whether – which of the two

Which – one of two or more

Witch – a woman with supernatural powers

Roots and Prefixes Bingo (page 45)

complain	detract	expand	prevent	reform
compose	disable	expect	preview	reject
conform	discharge	explain	probate	repack
conserve	discover	expose	process	replay
contest	display	extract	project	repose
contract	displease	incite	propose	reserve
convent	dispose	indict	protest	retail
converse	disserve	inform	protract	retell
debase	distract	inject	react	retest
debate	diverse	invent	rebate	retract
decent	enable	inverse	rebuild	reverse
deform	enact	percent	recent	review
deject	entail	perform	recess	unable
depose	exact	perverse	recharge	uncover
deserve	excess	predict	recite	unfair
detail	exchange	preserve	recover	unpack
detest	excite	pretest	refill	unsafe

70

Analogies Analysis

Possible Answers (page 49)

1. bottom
2. loud, noisy
3. grocery store, refrigerator
4. glove, mitten
5. write
6. think
7. liquid
8. peace, surrender
9. vegetable
10. go
11. carpenter, builder
12. him
13. tear, shred
14. sing
15. recipe
16. clock, watch
17. back
18. flour, bread
19. hive
20. poverty
21. solar system
22. sick, unhealthy
23. breakable, delicate
24. find, discover
25. happiness
26. calf
27. sad
28. finger
29. goal
30. play, theater
31. fly
32. cars
33. tree
34. foot
35. cook, bake, roast
36. taste, speak
37. stop
38. pounds, grams
39. triple
40. sun
41. road, track
42. fish
43. rough
44. ugly
45. science
46. calm
47. multiplication
48. eat

Smilin' Similes

Possible Answers (page 56)

As pretty as a picture
As fluffy as a cloud
Swims like a fish
As peaceful as a dove
As gentle as a lamb
As slippery as an eel
As busy as a bee
Sings like a bird

Sleeps like a baby
Fight like cats and dogs
As flat as a pancake
As deep as the ocean
As white as snow
As light as a feather
As cold as ice
Sinks like a stone

As strong as a horse
As rough as sandpaper
As black as night
Moves like a snail
As smooth as glass
As soft as silk
As tall as a flagpole
As sly as a fox

1. Head in the clouds – daydreaming or lost in thought

2. Right off the bat – immediately

3. Cold feet – lost his nerve or became afraid

4. Down in the dumps – sad or depressed

5. Tickled pink – very pleased or delighted

6. Hit the roof – to get angry suddenly

7. Pulled strings – secretly used some influence to get something

8. Keep a straight face – to keep from laughing

9. Out on a limb – take a risk

10. Red-carpet treatment – special treatment given to someone important

11. Break the ice – to reduce nervousness or tension in a situation

12. From soup to nuts – the whole thing, from start to finish

13. Eat your words – to take back what you said

14. Calls the shots – is in charge

15. Clammed up – refused to talk

16. Spitting image – an exact likeness

17. Back to square one – start at the beginning again because of failure

18. His bark is worse than his bite – he sounds more frightening than he behaves or acts

19. Wet blanket – someone who spoils the fun by being dull or depressing

20. Make waves – to cause trouble

21. Dark-horse candidate – a candidate whom people know little about but who unexpectedly wins

22. The last straw – the final problem of a series of other problems that is more than a person can bear

23. Took the rap – took the blame, especially by someone who is innocent

24. On cloud nine – very happy

25. Down the drain – lost forever

26. Keep under your hat – keep something secret

27. Hang in there – to continue without giving up

28. Green thumb – have a special talent for growing plants

29. Quick on the draw – quick to understand and answer questions

30. Monkey business – fooling around

31. Took a powder – left in a rush, as if to avoid getting caught

32. Cold shoulder – ignore completely

33. Tip of the iceberg – just a small part of an even bigger problem

34. Hit the books – study very carefully

35. Walking on air – to be very happy or elated

36. Burn the candle at both ends – to work very hard to the point of exhaustion

37. Piece of cake – a very easy task

38. With flying colors – with much success

39. On the fritz – not working

40. Green with envy – very jealous

41. For the birds – worthless

42. Cut the mustard – to be able to handle the job

43. Play second fiddle – to have a smaller role or be inferior to someone

44. Keep his chin up – to not show sadness or disappointment

45. Hit the nail right on the head – to be precisely right about something

46. Can't hold a candle to – is inferior to someone else

47. Jump down your throat – to scream at someone angrily

48. Spilled the beans – gave away a secret